JARROLD SHORT WALKS

leisure walks for all ages

North London

Compiled by
Leigh Hatts

D1391003

JARROLD
publishing

Mapping
sourced from

Ordnance
Survey®

Text: Leigh Hatts
Photography: Leigh Hatts
Editor: Crawford Gillan
Designer: Doug Whitworth

© Jarrold Publishing 2002

 This product includes mapping data licensed from Ordnance Survey ® with the permission of the Controller of Her Majesty's Stationery Office. © Crown Copyright 2002. All rights reserved. Licence number 100017593. Pathfinder is a registered trade mark of Ordnance Survey, the national mapping agency of Great Britain.

Jarrold Publishing ISBN0-7117-2090-8

While every care has been taken to ensure the accuracy of the route directions, the publishers cannot accept responsibility for errors or omissions, or for changes in details given. The countryside is not static: hedges and fences can be removed, field boundaries can alter, footpaths can be rerouted and changes in ownership can result in the closure or diversion of some concessionary paths. Also, paths that are easy and pleasant for walking in fine conditions may become slippery, muddy and difficult in wet weather, while stepping-stones across rivers and streams may become impassable.

If you find an inaccuracy in either the text or maps, please write or e-mail Jarrold Publishing at one of the addresses below.

First published 2002
by Jarrold Publishing

Printed in Belgium
by Proost NV, Turnhout. 1/02

Jarrold Publishing
Pathfinder Guides, Whitefriars,
Norwich NR3 1TR
E-mail: pathfinder@jarrold.com
www.jarroldpublishing.co.uk/
pathfinders

Front cover: Regent's Park
Previous page: Pillar box outside Harrow School

Contents

Keymap   4

Introduction   6

Walks

Short, easy walks

1   Smithfield   10
2   Bow Back Rivers   12
3   Highgate   15
4   Wapping   18
5   The Royal Parks   21
6   Regent's Park   24
7   Chigwell   27
8   Harrow   31

Walks of modest length, likely to involve some modest uphill walking

9   Stockley Park   34
10   Osterley   37
11   Hampton Court   40
12   Ruislip   43
13   Hampstead Heath   46
14   Lea Valley Walk   49
15   Denham   52
16   Marble Hill and Syon   56

More challenging walks which may be longer and/or over more rugged terrain, often with some stiff climbs

17   Epping Forest   60
18   Brent River Park   63
19   Mill Hill   67
20   Watford   71

Further Information   76
Walking Safety; Follow the Country Code;
Useful Organisations; Ordnance Survey Maps
Answers to Questions   80

Keymap

SCALE 1:250 000 or 1 INCH to 4 MILES *1CM to 2.5KM*

KILOMETRES

MILES

KEYMAP HEIGHTS SHOWN IN FEET

Introduction

The routes and information in this book have been devised specifically with families and children in mind. All the walks include points of interest as well as a question to provide an objective.

If you, or your children, have not walked before, choose from the shorter walks for your first outings, although none of the walks is especially demanding. The purpose is not simply to get from A to B, but to enjoy an exploration, which may be just a steady stroll in the countryside.

The walks are graded by length and difficulty, but few landscapes are truly flat, especially those among the Chilterns. Even short walks may involve some ascent, but this is nowhere excessive. Details are given under Route Features in the first information box for each route. The precise nature of the ground underfoot, however, will depend on recent weather conditions. If you do set out on a walk and discover the going is harder than you expected, or the weather has deteriorated, do not be afraid to turn back. The route will always be there another day, when you are fitter or the children are more experienced or the weather is better.

London countryside

London has plenty of countryside and it is easily reached. The countryside is not outside London it is inside. Within the M25 there are 96 farms and at least 6,800 head of cattle.

Cows are found at Mill Hill, where there are also horses, fields, farmshops and even beehives. Further south, cattle graze on the Thames-side meadow at Syon, where the natural creeks are washed twice daily by fresh water pushed back by the North Sea tide. Nearby, at Hampton Court and Bushey Parks, deer run free. Royal venison is sold in Smithfield, where there is a very different walk in the City of London's former 'smooth field'.

Royal deer are no longer found in Hyde Park or Regent's Park but this

The Millennium Bridge

countryside remains trapped in Central London, providing extraordinarily rewarding walks away from traffic. Both parks, enjoyed by many in summer, take on their old country mantle in autumn and winter when there are fewer visitors.

Use public transport

There is certainly no need to go far to find countryside. London's public transport network is extensive and the service compares very favourably with other parts of the country. Such places as Epping Forest, Hampton Court or the Buckinghamshire borders can easily be reached from Central London well within an hour.

Using public transport is strongly advised when you wish to go walking in London. Not only are London roads very crowded, with a notorious traffic jam record, but parking is very limited. Central London has been zoned for a congestion charge and many controlled parking zones have recently been introduced in London boroughs. Visitors to Southwark, for example, are advised not to arrive by car and the City, across the river, has implemented a 'severe traffic reduction' policy. This does, however, increase the pleasure of exploring on foot.

While many Underground stations on the edge of London have pay-and-display car parks, it should be noted that space is often limited on weekdays.

One Day or Weekend Travelcards, obtainable at Underground and mainline stations, are good value and allow all-day travel on buses, Underground and rail. The ticket is especially useful when walking one of the linear routes along the Thames or between stations.

String of villages

It is often suggested that London is really a string of villages which have joined up. This sense of village is found even on a walk which begins at London Bridge. Its climax is the old dockland Wapping village which retains its unique characteristics, including bridge entries which made the community into an island. Hampstead is in the Borough of Camden, which includes part of Covent Garden, but Hampstead village is still a reality, nestling alongside the vast Hampstead Heath. Nearby Highgate, being isolated on a hill, has an even greater village feel as it looks down on the rest of London.

Sampling long distance paths

This book offers an easy way to sample many long distance routes. Three central London walks include a section of the Thames Path national trail which links the capital with the Home Counties and beyond. The Lea Valley walk is almost entirely on the Lea Valley Path and occasionally on other routes it is possible to see the London Loop waymark indicating that the path is part of the 140-mile London Outer Orbital Path which circles Inner London.

There is plenty to discover and inspire within London and these walks enjoyed at different times will reveal varying seasons in all their splendour and allow for contrasting experiences.

London's growth

At first, London was just the City of London or what we today call the Square Mile where the City churches and financial institutions are found. The Tower of London, on the east side, was outside London – it is still outside the City – and Westminster, to the west, was a palace and a monastery on a triangular island created by the Thames on one side and the River Tyburn on the other two.

South London was not London but countryside later called Surrey. When Mary I prepared to return to London with her new husband, Philip of Spain, she went first to the country home of the Bishop of Winchester in Southwark. She went for a ride around the farmland before entering the capital by crossing London Bridge.

As late as 1689, William II was able to claim that he was moving to the country when he left Whitehall for Kensington Palace. Even in Queen Victoria's reign, London was said to end at Hyde Park Corner, where the Duke of Wellington lived. His house, being the first passed by a traveller arriving from the west, was known as 'Number One London', the first house on the capital's edge.

By the end of Victoria's reign there had been dramatic growth. The Metropolitan Police and the London County Council had both been established to operate with wide boundaries. Eventually, Middlesex was

Three Mills

embraced and by 1965 the present County of London boundary had been established, eating into the Home Counties, with 32 new large boroughs within this new Greater London area. This large circle is large enough to include many green spaces saved by the Corporation of London which, for more than a century, has pursued a policy of preserving outstanding countryside threatened with development. These and other green lungs long enjoyed by Londoners are now officially within London.

1 Smithfield

START	Blackfriars
DISTANCE	2 miles (3.2km)
TIME	1½ hours
PARKING	None
ROUTE FEATURES	Riverside path and City streets

This walk explores the medieval suburb behind the City of London and follows the line of the River Fleet, which is now covered by Farringdon Street and New Bridge Street, down to its confluence with the River Thames under Blackfriars Bridge. Smithfield is home not only to the famous hospital but to a church which has featured in films.

From the station turn left to start walking over Blackfriars Bridge. After a short distance go down steps on the left. Turn downstream to follow the riverside path under the railway bridge. At the Millennium Bridge turn inland up steps. Walk towards St Paul's Cathedral, crossing Queen Victoria Street on the way. At the next road, go left to reach the front of the cathedral.

Charterhouse Square covers a Black Death burial ground. The gateway, dating from 1405, was the entrance to a Carthusian monastery which became a mansion. Elizabeth I spent the week before her Coronation here and James VI of Scotland was proclaimed King James of England at the gate. In 1611 the complex became a school and almshouse. Charterhouse school is now in Surrey but the alms tradition continues with 60 single retired men living here as brothers.

A Continue to the top of Ludgate Hill and turn right into Ave Maria Lane. Walk to the far end of the street and, at Newgate Street, turn left to a crossroads by the Old Bailey. Turn right into Giltspur Street to pass the golden 'Fat Boy' on the left. At Smithfield, bear right past St Bartholomew's Hospital gateway to reach St Bartholomew the Great Church ahead.

PUBLIC TRANSPORT Underground or rail to Blackfriars station
REFRESHMENTS Pubs and cafés in Smithfield
PUBLIC TOILETS Opposite St Bartholomew's Church
ORDNANCE SURVEY MAPS Explorer 173 (London North)

St Bartholomew the Great is the surviving church of a priory founded in 1123 by Rahere, Henry I's court jester. The Augustinian monks' main task was running the next door hospital which is today known as St Bart's. The church lost its nave during Henry VIII's reign so today the congregation must sit in the facing seats in the Norman choir. The historic building has been used in many films, including the final marriage ceremony scene in *Four Weddings and a Funeral*.

B Walk down Cloth Fair at the side of the churchyard and church. At the Hand & Shears go left and pass under an arch by Ye Olde Red Cow. Cross the road to walk up Hayne Street, opposite Charterhouse Square. Go through the gates opposite into the cobbled area of the square to find the Charterhouse gateway.

Turn left to go through gates in the square's north-west corner and walk ahead along Charterhouse Street. At the far end, bear right to walk along the wide street with the main meat market buildings on the left.

C At the far end go left into Farringdon Street to walk under Holborn Viaduct. Pass the end of Fleet Street at Ludgate Circus and continue ahead along New Bridge Street to find Blackfriars station which is reached by a subway in front of the Blackfriar pub.

St Bartholomew the Great

Why is a turning off Farringdon Street, just beyond Holborn Viaduct, called Turnagain Lane?

2 *Bow Back Rivers*

START Bromley-by-Bow
DISTANCE 2 miles (3.2km)
TIME 1½ hours
PARKING Three Mill Lane
car park next to Tesco
(pay and display)
ROUTE FEATURES Waterside
footpaths

Three Mills, one of a group of islands on the River Lea, is a venue for film making. The first Big Brother TV series was set here on Mill Meads, once part of Stratford Langthorne Abbey. The islands are surrounded by the tidal Bow Back Rivers where reed beds provide a rare habitat. Swans, herons and sometimes kingfishers can be seen at low tide.

Three Mills, site of mills since Saxon times, once had four mills but now there are two. House Mill, built in 1776, is Britain's largest tide mill – driven by the water of the River Lea trapped upstream at high tide. Clock Mill was built in 1817 but its clock tower dates from at least 1750. Milling ceased in 1940 but House Mill can now be visited on summer Sunday afternoons. In the water at the southern end of the Prescott Channel are the remains of the Euston Arch used to hold back water at low tide.

At Bromley-by-Bow station go left down into the subway. On the far side turn sharp right to walk downhill with traffic to the left.

Bear right by Tesco down Three Mill Lane. Cross the River Lea to pass between the two mills. Ahead is Three Mills Film Studios. Turn left up a wide road to pass a bridge and keep forward on a path running between the Three Mills Wall River and fenced grass. There is also a lower path and, on the far side, there are usually house boats.

Ⓐ Go through a gate by a refurbished memorial to men killed in a well rescue in 1901. Cross the bridge and keep to the waterside along the backs of houses. At a main road, turn right past a bus stop and across a road junction.

PUBLIC TRANSPORT Underground to Bromley-by-Bow station
REFRESHMENTS Tesco in Three Mill Lane
PUBLIC TOILETS Three Mill Lane
ORDNANCE SURVEY MAPS Explorer 162 (Greenwich & Gravesend)

The **Abbey Mills Pumping Station**, on the Greenwich Meridian, was completed in 1865 to pump sludge from London's sewers. The mix of gothic and Italian styles along with a cruciform plan led to the building being called both the 'cathedral of sewage' and 'a monument to excrement'. Once it was flanked by tall flues disguised as Moorish towers. The Greenway alongside is on top of the Northern Outfall Sewer Embankment.

Well rescue memorial

Turn right into the Greenway and follow the high path as far as the Abbey Mills Pumping Station on the right.

B At the next junction go right and down a gentle slope. Where the path next divides, bear left to go down

to the waterside of Abbey Creek. Channelsea Island is opposite. Stay on this path, known as Long Wall Path, to reach the bridge over Prescott Channel. Behind are the gates leading to the *Big Brother* site.

C Turn left at the end of the bridge and follow the path along a painted wall as it bends into Bow Creek with a view of the mills.

Go through a gateway and over the railway lines. Turn left to cross the river and walk up Three Mill Lane. Turn left on to the rising main road to find at the top the pedestrian underpass leading to Bromley-by-Bow Station. ●

? *What is the Euston Arch?*

Clock Mill

Highgate

START Highgate
END Archway
DISTANCE 2 miles (3.2km)
TIME 1½ hours
PARKING Very limited at station
ROUTE FEATURES Village paths and roads

3

Highgate had a hilltop toll gate when the road over the hill was built in 1386. An early traveller was Dick Whittington who did not get to the top. Past residents include poets Samuel Taylor Coleridge, buried in St Michael's Church, and John Betjeman who remembered sheep here. Highgate, of course, offers views of the City to which Whittington returned.

At Highgate station ticket hall bear right to leave by the stairs leading to the car park. Follow the station road up to a junction and turn right to cross Archway Road. Go ahead up Jacksons Lane which runs steeply uphill to narrow dramatically. Where it widens, go right to cross Southwood Lane and walk up a passage known as Park Walk.

A Turn right to pass the Wrestlers where a plaque records the Swearing on the Horns ceremony still held here. Continue past number 92 with its Dickens plaque and across Castle Yard to pass the

Sir Sidney Waterlow

PUBLIC TRANSPORT Underground to Highgate station and from Archway station
REFRESHMENTS Lauderdale House in park
PUBLIC TOILETS Pond Square
ORDNANCE SURVEY MAPS Explorer 173 (London North)

Highgate School buildings. At the far end, opposite the Gatehouse, go left round the corner to cross

> **Lauderdale House** dates from Tudor times but is named after Lady Lauderdale who inherited the house in 1645. Samuel Pepys visited in 1660 just before the house was let to Nell Gwyn who threatened to throw her baby out of the window unless its father, Charles II, promised provision. Preacher John Wesley spent a night here in 1782 calling it 'one of the most elegant boarding houses in England'. It is now an art gallery and café.

the end of Southwood Lane. At once turn right to cross Highgate High Street and walk right for a short distance to find steps on the left leading down to Pond Square.

Go ahead to the far corner and past Tadpole Cottage to turn left into a flat road called West Hill. At the far end there is the Flask pub **B** on a corner. Left is Highgate Church and over to the right is a house, with plaques, where both Coleridge and JB Priestley lived.

Bear round to the left to walk back towards the village

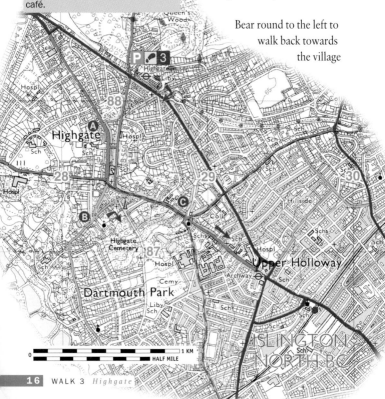

along South Grove. Go right down Swains Lane. Walk past a left turning but go left at a gateway into Waterlow Park.

Turn right and left. At the next path junction go right and at once bear left. There is a view down to a lake and soon there is a statue of Sir Sidney Waterlow on the left. Stay on the path to reach the back of Lauderdale House. Here, walk down the right side of the house, past the café, to reach the main road.

House on Highgate Hill

C At Lauderdale House gateway turn right to walk down Highgate Hill passing St Joseph's Church. Farther down the hill, just past the hospital and before the Whittington Stone pub, there is Whittington Stone. Continue down the hill to reach Archway station.

> **?** *What is on the Whittington Hospital sign?*

> The **Whittington Stone** marks the spot where Dick Whittington is said to have heard Bow Bells in the City of London calling him back. 'Turn again Whittington, thrice Lord Mayor of London' are the traditional words but, in fact, he became Mayor four times. Whittington, who came from Gloucestershire, was certainly on the wrong road home.

4 *Wapping*

START Wapping
DISTANCE 2 miles (3.2km)
TIME 1½ hours
PARKING Roadside parking in Wapping High Street
ROUTE FEATURES Riverside and dockside paths

Wapping's waterside has been opened up with promenades wide and narrow providing panoramic views of the great River Thames' landmarks such as Tower Bridge, Canary Wharf and Rotherhithe waterfront. Inland, the redundant docks have been converted into a canalside walk where new residents include ducks and The Times *newspaper.*

At the station turn right along Wapping High Street. After a short distance (almost opposite 131), go right up a slope and through a red gate to reach the riverside. The path runs through a second gate to St Hilda's Wharf before returning to the road along narrow New Crane Stairs.

Pass New Crane Wharf and go right into Wapping Wall. Just beyond the Prospect of Whitby Public House bear right to return to the river and find the entrance to Shadwell Basin. At the road, go right across the bridge and up Glamis Road with a view of St Mary's Church in Cable Street ahead.

When **London Docks** were built Wapping became an island village with drawbridges at all entries. Wapping High Street is of Elizabethan origin and by 1750 had 36 taverns to meet the needs of sailors and travellers. In 1688 Judge Jeffreys was captured at the Town of Ramsgate just before he was due to board a ship for France. The fuchsia was introduced to British gardens by a sailor who brought the first plant back to the Prospect of Whitby from the West Indies.

PUBLIC TRANSPORT Underground to Wapping
REFRESHMENTS The Town of Ramsgate and Prospect of Whitby in Wapping High Street and Wapping Wall
PUBLIC TOILETS None
ORDNANCE SURVEY MAPS Explorer 173 (London North)

A At the main road, The Highway, turn left to pass St Paul's Church. Stay on the main road to cross the end of Garnet Street. Turn left into traffic-free Queen Victoria Terrace. There is a small round building linked to the Underground line beneath. Soon there is grass to the left.

At a four-way junction turn right and follow the path with water to the left. The path and water drop down to pass under Wapping Lane. On the right there are tall mast ships in Tobacco Dock. Stay on the canalside path round two bends.

B At the third bend pass under the bridge and go up steps to

Charity children on an old school

Shadwell's St Paul's, standing high above Shadwell Basin, is known as the Sea Captains' Church. Navigator Captain James Cook was a parishioner and his son was baptised in the old church in 1763. Also christened here was Jane Randolph, mother of US President Thomas Jefferson.

A view of Tower Bridge from Wapping

Hermitage Basin. Bear left round the former dock so that the water is to the right. Go through gates at the far end and turn left along Wapping High Street.

At first, there is grass on the riverside. Go up the wide steps in the centre of Cinnabar Wharf to reach the riverside. Turn left downstream to follow the path back to the road. Turn right to continue along Wapping High Street. The road crosses Wapping Pierhead, a former dock entrance, before passing the Town of Ramsgate and the River Police Headquarters. Ahead is Wapping station.

> **?** *How long has the River Thames Police service been based in Wapping High Street?*

The Royal Parks

START Trafalgar Square
END Bayswater
DISTANCE 3½ miles (5.6km)
TIME 2 hours
PARKING None
ROUTE FEATURES Park paths

The string of Royal Parks between Whitehall and Kensington comprise 483 green acres in the heart of the capital. Hyde Park is large enough to lose the traffic noise and only the odd tall building on the skyline is a reminder of the encircling city. The route's climax is Kensington Palace where young Victoria became Queen.

From Trafalgar Square walk down Whitehall and through the Horse Guards entrance arch to reach Horse Guards Parade. Continue across the open space to the road and enter the gate to the left of the Guards Memorial.

Turn left and stay on the path as it passes Duck Island and bends with the water.

Cross the bridge and turn left. At the far end turn right

Kensington Palace

up to The Mall and cross directly over.

Ⓐ Keep to the right of the South Africa pillar ahead to walk round the back of the long curving balustrade with a view of Buckingham Palace. At the bottom of Constitution Hill take the straight path alongside the sandy horse ride and the cycle lane.

At the top, pass the Memorial Gate and use the

PUBLIC TRANSPORT Underground to Charing Cross and from Queensway
REFRESHMENTS Waterside café at Hyde Park's Serpentine
PUBLIC TOILETS At east end of St James's Park
ORDNANCE SURVEY MAPS Explorer 173 (London North)

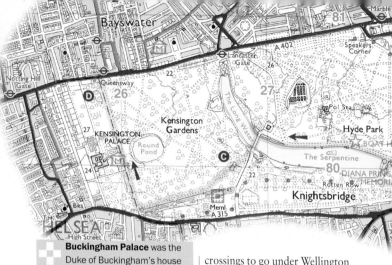

Buckingham Palace was the Duke of Buckingham's house before George III turned it into a family home. Queen Victoria made it the monarch's main residence. The famous façade with the balcony dates only from 1913, when George V was King. There are 600 rooms but the Queen and Prince Philip live in just a dozen on the north side.

crossings to go under Wellington Arch and enter Hyde Park under the archway marked Hyde Park Corner. Keep forward to cross a park road and, at once, turn left. Sandy Rotten Row is on the left. After passing the Rose Garden, take the second turning on the

Green Park

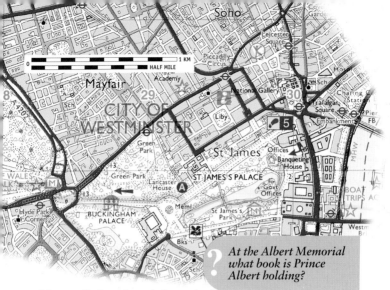

At the Albert Memorial what book is Prince Albert holding?

right to walk along the end of The Serpentine.

B At The Dell restaurant turn left to follow the waterside path. Stay by the water to go under the bridge to the Long Water. At once take the rustic steps on the right. Turn right through a gateway and cross the bridge. On the far side, go right through a gateway. Turn left and then right to reach the Serpentine Gallery.

C Go round two sides of the Gallery building and then bear half right aross two junctions before arriving behind the Albert Memorial.

Continue on the path ahead, with a railing on the left. On reaching the Broad Walk, turn right. The wide path rises to pass between Kensington Palace and the Round Pond.

D Later, there is, to the left, the Diana, Princess of Wales Memorial Playground. At the end, cross Bayswater Road and go right to turn left into Queensway and find Queensway station on the left. ●

Kensington Palace became a royal residence when William III moved from Whitehall to enjoy the pure country air which he hoped would alleviate his asthma. Edward VIII called the Palace 'the aunt heap' because so many of his relatives lived there. Recent residents have included Diana, Princess of Wales, and Princess Margaret.

6 Regent's Park

START Regent's Park
DISTANCE 2 miles (3.2km)
TIME 2 hours
PARKING None
ROUTE FEATURES Parkland paths, including a steep climb

Regent's Park provides a rural buffer between the Oxford Street and Marylebone shops and north London. In the 17th and 18th centuries it was farmland providing London's milk. Walking in the park is particularly rewarding in spring when daffodils mass the banks of the lake. Dogs are not allowed on part of this walk, including the Primrose Hill viewpoint.

Turn left from Regent's Park Station. At the road junction go right over the crossing and into Park Square West. Keep forward past a modern postbox and cross the Outer Circle road to enter the main park.

Regent's Park has been open as a public park since 1841, soon after the 'wedding cake' style houses designed by John Nash had been built around the edge. The lake abounds with ducks and swans both black and white. The Inner Circle, once the Royal Botanic Society Garden, is now Queen Mary's Rose Garden. The northern part of the park is occupied by London Zoo which opened in 1828.

Turn left onto a path running along the edge of the park. Cross a road at York Gate, with St Marylebone Church to the left. The path continues by the lake. Pass Clarence Bridge and continue to the far end where there is a café, boathouse and a view of the mosque.

A Bear right to cross two bridges. Go half left on the path signed Primrose Hill Bridge. The path runs over a large expanse of grass to a gateway. Cross the Outer Circle road and go ahead on a path by a running track to reach the bridge over the Regent's Canal.

PUBLIC TRANSPORT Underground to Regent's Park
REFRESHMENTS Park cafés
PUBLIC TOILETS At north end off lake
ORDNANCE SURVEY MAPS OS Explorer 173 (London North)

At the road go right to the crossing and, on the far side, enter Primrose Hill by a lodge. Take the left hand path up the hill and, at the second junction, go right to reach the viewpoint.

The boating lake island

B Leave the top by taking the path to the left downhill. Where the path divides take the left hand

> **Why is this parkland called Regent's Park?**

The 206 foot high **Primrose Hill**, which once abounded with primroses, was cleared of trees in Elizabeth I's reign and ever since it has been a viewpoint. More recent landmarks to be seen are the Crystal Palace radio mast and Canary Wharf. In the Second World War an anti-aircraft battery was on the summit.

path on both occasions to reach the far south-eastern corner. Cross the road and at once turn left along Prince Albert Road. Once level with St Mark's Church, go right to cross the canal and the Outer Circle and join the almost mile long Broad Walk. At first, London Zoo is on the right. Ahead is a white drinking fountain.

C Stay on the straight path to cross Chester Road and pass through formal gardens.

Just before the next road, turn left past a fountain to follow a path which curves to a road junction. Cross the road to walk down Park Square East ahead. At the main road, cross the dual carriageway at the crossing and go right to reach Regent's Park station. ●

A Regent's Park house

● Historic church and pub ● viewpoint ● farmland

Chigwell

START Chigwell
DISTANCE 2½ miles (4km)
TIME 2 hours
PARKING Roadside parking near station
ROUTE FEATURES Footpaths which may be muddy

7

Charles Dickens thought that 'rural' Chigwell was 'the greatest place in the world'. In the early 20th century the steam milk train would stop between Grange Hill and Chigwell stations to collect fruit and vegetables from the Great Eastern Railway's own farm for use in the kitchens of the Great Eastern Hotel at Liverpool Street station.

🥾 Turn right out of Chigwell station and walk down the road past the shops. The road crosses the Chigwell Brook to climb out of the valley to Chigwell Church **A**.

Continue on the right hand side,

Buried in **Chigwell churchyard** is George Shillibeer who, in 1829, pioneered the London bus service with a horse-drawn route from Marylebone to the City. (He is on the left of the main path just after the surface changes from gravel to grass.) Also here is John Knight (at the back opposite west door) of Knight's Castile soap fame. Charles Dickens used the King's Head as the model for the Maypole in *Barnaby Rudge*.

past the King's Head and Chigwell School up the village street. At Vicarage Lane cross over to find a footpath running down the lane's left side. After a short distance, go left along a fenced path. Cross a school approach road to a gap and a field. Bear half right across the centre to the far corner. Chigwell Row Church can be seen in the distance.

Go right over a junction of country lanes and down Green Lane. Soon there is a signpost **B** pointing to the Pudding Lane viewpoint just over ¼ mile away. The main walk continues ahead on Green Lane,

PUBLIC TRANSPORT Underground to Chigwell
REFRESHMENTS Pubs in village
PUBLIC TOILETS None
ORDNANCE SURVEY MAPS Explorer 174 (Epping Forest & Lee Valley)

which opens out on reaching a house. Hillside is on the corner as

Pudding Lane Viewpoint is 250 feet above sea level and has views back to London with the BT Tower and Canary Wharf visible on clear days. To the north, is Epping Forest and just beyond the motorway is the Bank of England printworks.

the lane bears right to meet Vicarage Lane.

Turn right on the pavement ready to cross the road with care once opposite a pavement. Continue past weatherboarded houses to the next corner. Go left to pass between the last white cottage and a cottage with pointed windows.

The footpath does a double bend before running ahead by a ditch on the left. To the right, there is a view of Chigwell, with Buckhurst Hill behind. Stay by the field boundary as the path gently descends. At the bottom, the path turns sharp left to a junction. Go right to follow the side of the next field. There is a cemetery to the left and sometimes the rising path is behind trees. At the far end, go ahead on a straight path leading to the top of the railway embankment.

C The path bears right with the railway and then, after passing a

Chigwell village

Chigwell Church

bridge, right again. Once in the open, cross a track leading from gates. The path runs ahead with a ditch and hedge to the right. Chigwell Hall, with its tall chimneys, can be seen ahead. At the top of a slope, by field boundaries, keep to the left of a hedge ahead to go downhill to cross the Chigwell Brook. Turn left along Courtland Drive. At the main road, go left uphill to Chigwell station.

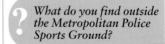

? *What do you find outside the Metropolitan Police Sports Ground?*

Harrow

START Harrow-on-the-Hill

DISTANCE 1½ miles (2.4km)

TIME 2 hours

PARKING Shopping centre car park (pay & display)

ROUTE FEATURES Surfaced paths and steep climb

8

Harrow-on-the-Hill, topped with its church spire, has been a landmark for more than 550 years. Charles Lamb pointed out to William Wordsworth that, at 400 feet, this made the spire higher than the one at Salisbury Cathedral. The village is isolated but still convenient for the shopping centre and station below, as this short walk will demonstrate.

Leave Harrow-on-the-Hill station by turning left at the ticket barrier and going down steps. Walk ahead up the road and go over the main road ahead. There is a crossing to the right. Continue ahead up Lansdowne Road. At the top, there is a junction of footpaths. Keep forward on the path signed 'The Hill' and running over the grass and up the side of the house. At the top, by the wood, a metalled path joins from the left.

> **Harrow Church** was founded by Archbishop Lanfranc in 1087 and had the spire added in 1450. In the churchyard is the Peachey tomb called the 'Peachey Stone' by the poet Byron who as a Harrow schoolboy 'mused the twilight hours away' gazing at the view which, on a clear day, includes the Chiltern Hills.

Here, there is a good view north-east over towards Stanmore.

Go right along an enclosed path. At a road go left. The steep way narrows to run through the extended churchyard and reach Byron's viewpoint.

Turn left to follow the path past the church to a lychgate. Once through the gate, go sharp left to walk below the church's east end. Ahead

PUBLIC TRANSPORT Underground to Harrow-on-the-hill

REFRESHMENTS Pub and teashop in village

PUBLIC TOILETS At station

ORDNANCE SURVEY MAPS OS Explorer 173 (London North)

Harrow School, with 770 boys, was founded in 1572 by a farmer who obtained a charter from Elizabeth I. Five prime ministers have been pupils, including Sir Winston Churchill, who often returned to hear school songs sung in the Speech Room. The prominent Vaughan Library and chapel were designed by George Gilbert Scott in the 19th century. Dramatist Richard Sheridan, who was a Harrow schoolboy in the 1760s, later lived at The Grove behind the church.

is The Grove. Follow the path downhill to pass Sheridan's stables.

A Turn right along the road, Grove Hill. At the junction with the High Street there is a plaque on the left hand corner.

Continue ahead along the High Street. After passing between the Harrow School Book Shop and the Outfitters, bear off to the right down West Street to pass the Tearoom. Continue past the Castle pub.

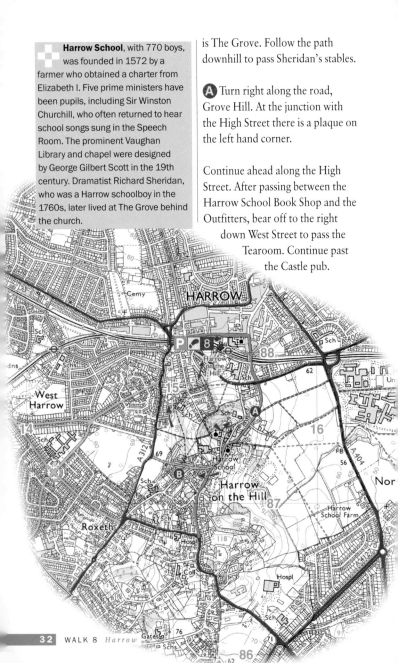

A Harrow School building

B By number 69 turn right into a footpath. Beyond a double bend follow the metalled path as it runs over a corner of the hill with fine views.

> **?** *What does the plaque record on the corner of Grove Hill at the end of the High Street?*

At a path junction go right along a wider path to pass a school and St Mary and St Thomas of Canterbury Church. Cross Roxborough Park Road and, at the end of the path, go left to follow the outward route by the grass down Lansdowne Road. Cross the main road to reach Harrow-on-the-Hill station.

●

9 Stockley Park

START	West Drayton
DISTANCE	3½ miles (5.6km)
TIME	2 hours
PARKING	West Drayton station (pay and display)
ROUTE FEATURES	Canal towpath and gravel park paths

In the 19th century, bricks were made at West Drayton. Later, empty clay pits were filled with rubbish. But between 1984 and 1993 new topsoil was added and more than a million trees planted. Worms were added to increase fertility. The award-winning Stockley Park is slowly maturing with the number of butterflies and birds increasing annually.

St Martin's Church at West Drayton is mainly 15th-century with traces of the 13th-century building which succeeded a Saxon Church. Next to the church is a Tudor gateway built as the entrance to the home of Henry VIII's Secretary of State, Sir William Paget. Elizabeth I rode through the arch just a year before her death. When West Drayton station opened in 1838 it was the first stop on the Great Western Railway after Paddington.

Turn right out of the station road to walk up the High Street. Once across the canal bridge, immediately go right at Horton Road and sharp right down to the canal. Turn left along the towpath. Pass under Horton Bridge and stay on the towpath to go under Iron Bridge Road, Stockley Bridge and the new Starveall Bridge, carrying a main road.

A Between the bend on the canal and the next bridge look for an entrance to Stockley Park set back on the left. Go through the kissing gate and ahead on the narrow gravel path which soon runs over

? *What is the centre of the new Stockley Park bridge reserved for?*

PUBLIC TRANSPORT Rail to West Drayton
REFRESHMENTS Pub at station and near end of route
PUBLIC TOILETS None
ORDNANCE SURVEY MAPS Explorer 172 (Chiltern Hills East) and 160 (Windsor)

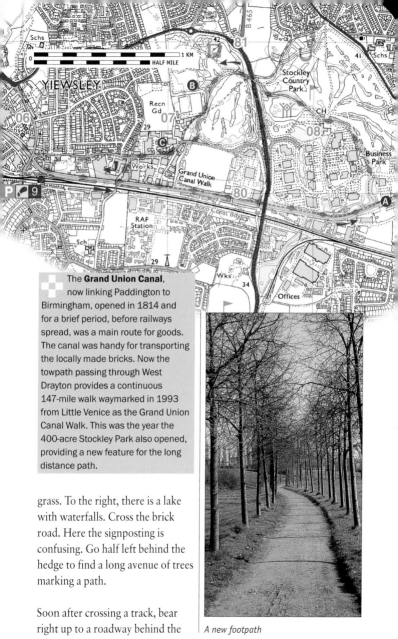

The **Grand Union Canal**, now linking Paddington to Birmingham, opened in 1814 and for a brief period, before railways spread, was a main route for goods. The canal was handy for transporting the locally made bricks. Now the towpath passing through West Drayton provides a continuous 147-mile walk waymarked in 1993 from Little Venice as the Grand Union Canal Walk. This was the year the 400-acre Stockley Park also opened, providing a new feature for the long distance path.

grass. To the right, there is a lake with waterfalls. Cross the brick road. Here the signposting is confusing. Go half left behind the hedge to find a long avenue of trees marking a path.

Soon after crossing a track, bear right up to a roadway behind the

A new footpath

Grand Union Canal

golf clubhouse. Go left and right up the side of the clubhouse. The path runs gently uphill and through the edge of a young wood. At a path junction, bear left to go over the bridge spanning a main road. Keep on the main track uphill. At the top there is a grass slope with seats on top for those wishing to enjoy the view.

B The walk continues on the path past the viewpoint. Bear left at a fork. Ignore two turnings to the right but look out for a London Loop waymark at the next turning on the right. This leads down to a kissing gate by a bus stop. (*If the path opposite is open it is possible to go directly to the canal and turn right for West Drayton.*)

C The main walk continues to the right along the road. When level with a café, go left down Horton Bridge Road to pass the Brickmakers Arms. At the canal bridge, go over to the right and down steps to the water. Turn right along the canal path. Just before the next bridge, go right through the kissing gate and over the bridge to walk down to West Drayton station.

Osterley

START Osterley
DISTANCE 3½ miles (5.6km)
TIME 2 hours
PARKING Osterley House car park
ROUTE FEATURES Parkland roads and footpaths which can be muddy

Osterley Park is a remarkable oasis wedged between the A4 and M4. Suddenly, the suburban houses stop and there is farmland allowing the visitor to imagine what this part of ancient Middlesex was like until the 20th century. Here, cattle and horses graze and rabbits are a familiar sight. There is even a farm shop.

Turn left out of Osterley station to walk along the main road. Go left into Thornbury Road and, at the end, enter the Osterley Park main gateway.

A Walk up the left side of the avenue, passing the Farm Shop halfway down on the right hand side. At the end, where the drive

Osterley station, opened in 1934, is a fine example of architect Charles Holden's work for the Underground and was inspired by his visit to Holland. The original 1883 Osterley and Spring Grove station in Thornbury Road is now the Osterley Bookshop.

Osterley Park lake

PUBLIC TRANSPORT Underground to Osterley
REFRESHMENTS Café next to Osterley House
PUBLIC TOILETS Alongside Osterley House café
ORDNANCE SURVEY MAPS Explorer 173 (London North)

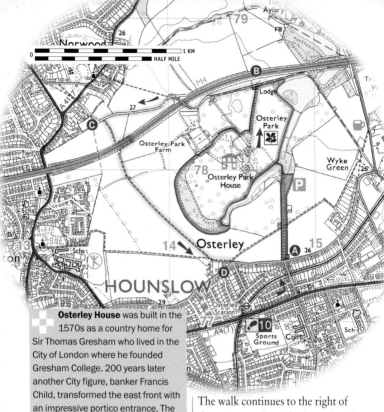

Osterley House was built in the 1570s as a country home for Sir Thomas Gresham who lived in the City of London where he founded Gresham College. 200 years later another City figure, banker Francis Child, transformed the east front with an impressive portico entrance. The house and grounds are now in the care of the National Trust.

turns left, keep forward past a gate and follow the path round a lake. Where the way divides, stay with the water to the left. *Only go through the gate ahead to view the west side of the mansion from the Great Meadow.*

> **?** *Why is the lodge called Jubilee Lodge?*

The walk continues to the right of the gate, round two further sides of the Cedar Lawn. Turn left to pass the east side of the house with its flight of steps. Ahead is the tearoom. Bear half right past the stable block to a gateway. At the divide beyond, go right and follow the wide path. On the left, there is a triangular field with a pond in the middle. At the far end is a lodge.

B Go through the gate and turn left along a wide, rough country track known as Osterley Lane.

To the left, there is the north side of the triangular field. At the end go through a gateway, past another Osterley entrance and follow the now metalled lane over the M4. Where the pavement ends, walk on the right hand side to face any traffic.

C In the centre of a gentle double bend go left on to a footpath signed 'Jersey Road and Osterley'. The fenced path runs straight ahead before bearing left to a long bridge spanning the M4.

Once on the far side, the way bears left. Ignore all turnings and follow the main track through thin trees.

Occasionally, there are numbered posts to indicate the way. There is a field boundary to the left and a large field, often used for grazing horses, to the right. After half a mile, the path is joined by another before entering a large field. On the right is an old wall.

D *At another junction only go left to visit the farm shop again or return to the car park.* The main walk continues over the low stile in the wall and up Bassett Gardens opposite. Turn right and look for a footpath sign next to number 102 on the left. A path leads to the main road. Go left for Osterley station. ●

Osterley House

● Parkland ● ponds ● palace ● deer

11 *Hampton Court*

START Hampton Wick
DISTANCE 3½ miles (5.6km)
TIME 2 hours
PARKING Kingston's main car park (pay & display) on south bank or Bushey Park car park on walk
ROUTE FEATURES Surfaced and grass parkland paths

Hampton Court and Bushey Parks were enclosed by Henry VIII who stocked them with deer which are still roaming freely. Hampton Court Park's Long Water and Bushey Park's ponds both attract swans and ducks. The public has been welcome to enjoy the 1,099 acres ever since Henry VIII's death in 1547.

Turn left out of Hampton Wick station to reach Kingston Bridge. The walk starts at the gateway to Hampton Court Park, next to the Bridge and the Old King's Head. Follow the park road and use the gate by the cattle grid.

As **Hampton Wick** was a hamlet far from the parish church west of the palace, a chapel, the present St John's, was built in 1831 on land given by its architect Edward Lapidge. The clock was added in 1834 so the little church on the edge of the parkland was new when young Queen Victoria came to the throne in 1837.

Keep right at the divide where a sign points to 'golf course'. At the second divide, go left on the road signed 'golf club and farm cottages'.

A On coming level with a pond, just before a crossroads, go right up the grass slope to the Long Water. Hampton Court Palace can be seen at the far end. Keeping the water to the right, walk the length of the stretch of water.

Over to the right, Hampton Wick Pond can be seen, while on high ground to the left is an ice house.

PUBLIC TRANSPORT Train to Hampton Wick
REFRESHMENTS Pubs or café at Hampton Court
PUBLIC TOILETS Hampton Court
ORDNANCE SURVEY MAPS OS Explorer 161 (London South)

At the end, bear left with a fence to find a gateway leading to a bridge over the ornamental water. Beyond the bridge, head for the palace ahead. Bear right on to the Broad Walk to keep the palace to the left. After passing the Royal Tennis Court, turn left through a gateway and bear half right through a garden called The Wilderness, known for its spring display of daffodils. The path leads to the Lion Gate where the Maze and the King's Arms are to the left.

The Wilderness in spring

Cross the main road to enter Bushey Park opposite. Follow the path, which bears away from the road on the left. After passing water on the right, the path ahead is over grass. To the right is the Diana Fountain, surrounded by water and ringed by a road.

B On reaching a car park and refreshment caravan, turn right to

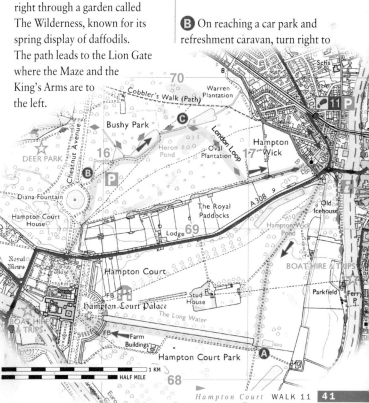

Deer in Hampton Court Park

walk along the side of the car park. Soon the car park on the left gives way to a small pond which opens out to Heron Pond. At the eastern end, follow the channel linking the water with Leg of Mutton Pond.

C On reaching this final pond, at once bear half right on a path which just misses the trees to the right. Stay on this path, which runs to the far south-eastern corner. Cross a metalled path to walk between the cricket ground fence

Why is the Bushey Park fountain called the Diana Fountain?

Hampton Court was built by Cardinal Thomas Wolsey who employed 500 servants. He gave the palace to Henry VIII who brought five of his six wives to the country retreat. His daughter Elizabeth I liked to celebrate Christmas here where mistletoe grows in the trees. William IV started guided tours and Queen Victoria opened the rooms for free viewing soon after her accession.

and a brick wall to a gateway in the corner. Follow a long avenue to a second gate opposite St John's Church at Hampton Wick. Turn right and left to reach the roundabout at Kingston Bridge. Continue to bear left up the High Street to reach Hampton Wick station.

Ruislip

12

START Ruislip
DISTANCE 4 miles (6.4km)
TIME 2½ hours
PARKING Ruislip station
(pay and display)
ROUTE FEATURES Woodland
paths

In Ruislip a vast lake surrounded by woodland offers a wonderful escape from the city centre, especially on a hot day or in autumn. The walk from the station to and from the Lido, with its sandy beach, is a pleasure as it passes up the High Street by picturesque buildings clustered around the church and through a monastic farm site.

Ruislip has a country church dating from the 13th century and complete with impressive medieval wall paintings. The dedication to St Martin of Tours is an indication that the patron was the French Abbey of Bec who held the nearby manor farm. Here, the main barn is not only as old as the church but the oldest in the country, hinting at its foundation by Bec Abbey.

Walk ahead from the station and turn left to a crossroads. Go right up the High Street. At the far end, by the church, go ahead down the gated road by the toilets. (There is a crossing round to the right.)

A The traffic-free road runs through the former Manor Farm. Just past the duck pond on the left, there is a farmyard. Keep forward to pass between stables and the farmhouse. The narrow path runs down the side of the Winston Churchill Hall to join its access road. Bear half left across the grass to the bridge spanning the River Pinn. Cross the road to continue on a short woodland path opposite which winds round to meet the end

? *At the farmyard what is the newest building called and why?*

PUBLIC TRANSPORT Underground to Ruislip
REFRESHMENTS Cafés and pub at Lido
PUBLIC TOILETS In village and by the Lido beach
ORDNANCE SURVEY MAPS OS Explorer 173 (London North)

of Sherwood Avenue.
Follow this residential
road across two
junctions to enter Park
Wood at the far end.

Walk up the pathway.
Take the left hand path
and ignore all turnings.
The way, shared with
horses, rises gently
through the trees.
Soon after crossing
a long, wide ride the
path ahead drops
down to a gateway by
the Lido. To the right
is the Lido's Woody
Park railway station.

B Turn left along the
promenade by the beach.
At the far end go up to a
gateway and turn right along
the high path on the western
bank. Go right at the end to

The Lido was dug in 1811 as a
reservoir feeder for the Grand
Union Canal. Park Wood supplied oak
in early Tudor times for the Tower of
London, the Palace of Westminster
and Windsor Castle. The 1¼ mile
narrow gauge railway opened in 1945
and now runs from Woody Bay to
Water's Edge carrying around 50,000
passengers a year in mainly diesel
hauled trains.

pass in front of
the Water's Edge pub.
Afterwards, the metalled path
turns inland to join a wider path
and reach Water's Edge station.
The path continues parallel to the
water. Beyond a gate the surface is

rough and, after a bend, the way is alongside the railway again. After Haste Hill station go ahead over the hidden bridge, spanning a stream, at the far end of the field. **C** The path bends round to the south with the railway, to run down the Lido's wooded east bank.

Ruislip Lido beach

On reaching the railway terminus and the beach, turn inland to retrace the outward route up through the woods. Keep ahead to go down Sherwood Avenue and the short path at the end to reach the road crossing the River Pinn. Go half left over the grass and up the path by Winston Churchill Hall and through Manor Farm. Keep forward past the church and down the High Street. At the bottom, go left into Pembroke Road to find Ruislip station on the right.

Park Wood in spring

13 *Hampstead Heath*

START Hampstead
DISTANCE 4 miles (6.4km)
TIME 2½ hours
PARKING None
ROUTE FEATURES Heathland paths and woodland lane

Hampstead has long attracted writers, including Keats, who met fellow poet Coleridge on the Heath. A chain of ponds includes the Ladies' Bathing Pond, where actress Margaret Rutherford swam every morning. This has always been considered a healthy place and even judges slept here under canvas to avoid London's Great Plague of 1665.

At Hampstead station go left to walk down Hampstead High Street. Turn left at Downshire Hill and at St John's Chapel bear right into Keats Grove to pass Keats House on the right.

At the far end, cross the main road and walk ahead onto the Heath. At the T-junction go left and soon bear round to the right to pass alongside the Hampstead Ponds.

A After the second pond, turn right and, on the far side of the water, follow a curving path uphill. Keep left at a fork. On emerging from the cutting, turn right. Keep

Hampstead is a hillside village which became fashionable when spa water was discovered in 1698. The first of many writers to be associated with the village was Samuel Johnson who came to stay in 1745. Its first commuter was artist John Constable, who lived in Flask Walk and had his studio in central London. Just off delightful Downshire Hill is Keats' House where the poet wrote his *Ode to a Nightingale* in the garden.

ahead through the wood and over path junctions. Ahead in the distance can be seen the spire of Highgate Church. Once in the open, the path runs downhill to Highgate Ponds.

PUBLIC TRANSPORT Underground to Hampstead
REFRESHMENTS Kenwood House café
PUBLIC TOILETS Kenwood House
ORDNANCE SURVEY MAPS Explorer 173 (London North)

At the bottom, bear left to walk alongside the pond and at the end bear right to walk between the two ponds. As the way forks, go left uphill and past a gate. Go left to join Millfield Lane.

B Soon there is the entrance to Kenwood Ladies' Bathing Pond. Stay in the lane, which later leaves the ponds to run uphill. At the top, where the lane turns right, go left

In the 18th century, **Kenwood House** was the country home of the Lord Chief Justice, Lord Mansfield, whose London house was in Bloomsbury. The art treasures include works by Hampstead artist George Romney as well as Vermeer's *Guitar Player*, stolen in 1974 but safely returned. The house is open daily, free of charge. The River Fleet rises on the lawn. The nearby Spaniards Inn is at least 400 years old and has welcomed Keats, Shelley, Byron and Dickens.

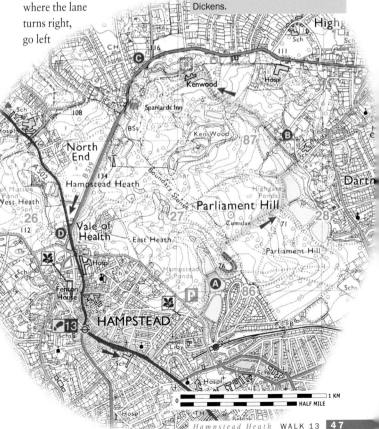

Kenwood House

through a gateway into the grounds of Kenwood House.

Turn right and walk towards the mansion. Pass along the garden front of the house and, at the orangery, go right through an ivy tunnel to reach the mansion's main entrance. On leaving the house, bear left to follow the drive to a road.

C Turn left along the road, past a bus stop, and uphill to pass the Spaniards Inn where the former tollhouse still narrows the road. Continue ahead along the raised straight road through woodland. Occasionally, there are glimpses to the left of Highgate Church and later the Dome, Canary Wharf and the City's tall buildings.

D At the junction by Jack Straw's Castle, bear left past Whitestone Pond and continue downhill to follow Heath Street to Hampstead station. ●

? What should motorists look out for between the Spaniards Inn and Whitestone Pond?

Lea Valley Walk

START Ponders End
END Tottenham Hale
DISTANCE 4 miles (6.4km)
TIME 3 hours
PARKING Roadside parking near station
ROUTE FEATURES Canal towpath and meadow

14

The Lea Valley runs from Hertfordshire down into London's East End. The River Lea rises at Luton and flows into the Thames opposite the Dome as seen on television's EastEnders. *This walk, in the confusingly named Lee Valley Park, offers the chance to see swans. Indeed, the swan is the logo of the Lea Valley Walk.*

The Ponder family lived at **Ponders End** in the 14th century. The weatherboarded flourmill, dating from 1789, is run by a sixth generation producing Wright's flour and bread mixes. East Mill House is early Georgian. In the 19th century this remote area saw electrical inventor Sir Joseph Swan work on his light bulb invention and Sir James Dewar invent the thermos flask, later manufactured in Tottenham.

Cross the main road using the high footbridge from the station to reach Mill Lodge at the entrance to the mill. Continue ahead along

Tottenham Lock waymark

PUBLIC TRANSPORT Rail (WAGN) to Ponders End and rail or Underground from Tottenham Hale
REFRESHMENTS Water's Edge Pub and Café at Stonebridge Lock
PUBLIC TOILETS None
ORDNANCE SURVEY MAPS Explorer 173 (London North) or 174 (Epping Forest & Lee Valley)

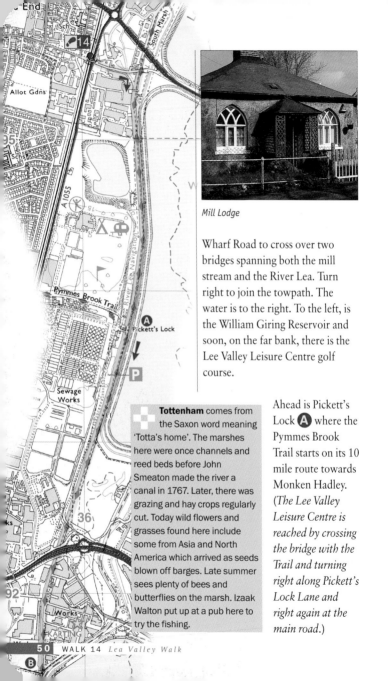

Mill Lodge

Wharf Road to cross over two bridges spanning both the mill stream and the River Lea. Turn right to join the towpath. The water is to the right. To the left, is the William Giring Reservoir and soon, on the far bank, there is the Lee Valley Leisure Centre golf course.

Ahead is Pickett's Lock **A** where the Pymmes Brook Trail starts on its 10 mile route towards Monken Hadley. (*The Lee Valley Leisure Centre is reached by crossing the bridge with the Trail and turning right along Pickett's Lock Lane and right again at the main road.*)

Tottenham comes from the Saxon word meaning 'Totta's home'. The marshes here were once channels and reed beds before John Smeaton made the river a canal in 1767. Later, there was grazing and hay crops regularly cut. Today wild flowers and grasses found here include some from Asia and North America which arrived as seeds blown off barges. Late summer sees plenty of bees and butterflies on the marsh. Izaak Walton put up at a pub here to try the fishing.

The main walk continues on the towpath. At the end of the reservoir there is a path signed to Chingford and the view across the water is of a tall refuse incineration chimney. Pass under a bridge and then a series of new road bridges known as the Lee Valley Viaduct. The towpath is then part of a road by the Lee Valley Trading Estate.

B At Chalk Bridge, where the scene changes dramatically, go up a slope to leave the towpath and cross the water. The bridge leads directly onto the remains of Tottenham Marshes. At once, go left along a straight grass path. The river is over to the left. Later, the path is alongside a fence before reaching a gateway and passing along the back of the Water's Edge Pub and Café.

C At nearby Stonebridge Lock, the towpath crosses from the far side. Continue south on the wide promenade-style towpath which also has water, the Pymmes Brook, sometimes visible to the right. On the far bank there are usually houseboats moored. Immediately after Tottenham Lock, go up the slope to a road.

> **?** *What does Hale mean in Tottenham Hale Station?*

Turn right along Ferry Road, crossing the end of Mill Mead Road, to walk uphill to cross the railway bridge. Keep on the pavement round to the right, or use the short-cut steps, to reach Tottenham Hale station.

● Lakes ● woods ● canal towpath ● pretty village

15 *Denham*

START Denham
DISTANCE 4 miles (6.4km)
TIME 2½ hours
PARKING Denham station (pay & display)
ROUTE FEATURES Canal towpath and village paths

The 69-acre Denham Country Park straddles the London boundary which is itself the delightful River Colne. Here in the Colne Valley there are herons, kingfishers and dragonflies on the river, canal and lakes. Denham has been described as 'one of the most attractive villages in the country' and featured in several films.

The **Denham Film Studios** may have closed but many stars still live in the village. The church even featured in *Carry on Matron*. Inside is a brass to Agnes Jordan, the last Abbess of Syon, and a bust of Sir Roger Hill who had Denham Place built during Mary II's reign. Ian Hendry was filmed outside the mansion when playing Lord Croxley in *The Persuaders*. In the main street there is Blacksmith's Cottage and three pubs.

At Denham station both platforms have steps leading down to the footpath in the tunnel below. Go left on the path which runs into the open and behind gardens. At the end, turn left into Savay Lane.

At the crossroads, go right into Moorfield Road.

At Green Bridge, spanning the River Colne which marks the London boundary, there is a view of an island in the river and a lake. Later the road passes the Horse and Barge pub which lies within the London Borough of Hillingdon. Continue ahead over the canal bridge **A** by Widewater Lock to reach the edge of South Harefield.

Immediately, having passed Widewater Place buildings on the right and before Dellside, go right

PUBLIC TRANSPORT Rail to Denham
REFRESHMENTS Fran's Tea Garden at Denham Deep Lock
PUBLIC TOILETS Colne Valley Park Visitor Centre
ORDNANCE SURVEY MAPS OS Explorer 172 (Chiltern Hills East)

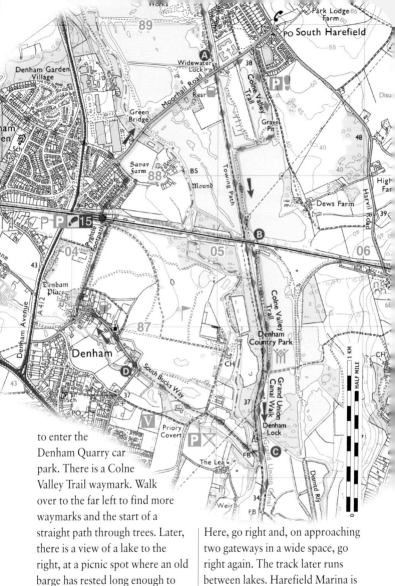

to enter the
Denham Quarry car
park. There is a Colne
Valley Trail waymark. Walk
over to the far left to find more
waymarks and the start of a
straight path through trees. Later,
there is a view of a lake to the
right, at a picnic spot where an old
barge has rested long enough to
have young trees sprouting from
inside. Soon the path joins a former
gravel workings track.

Here, go right and, on approaching
two gateways in a wide space, go
right again. The track later runs
between lakes. Harefield Marina is
to the right. Turn south with the
path, which now runs between a
lake to the left, and the canal.

An old barge in Denham Country Park

The path runs under the railway
B and past an anglers' lake.

On reaching a gateway at the end
of the lake, go right across a short
bridge to the canal. Cross the high
canal bridge to continue walking
south by the canal. The water is to
the left. Pass over the River Colne
and through Denham Deep Lock.

C After a short distance, turn
right on a path leading away from
the canal and across a high
footbridge, with steps, spanning
the River Colne. The bridge leads

from London to Buckinghamshire.
The path bears round to the right.
Go through a kissing gate and
follow the path ahead, which at
first is a causeway between ponds.

This section of the **Grand
Union Canal** opened in 1797,
linking Brentford with Hemel
Hempstead. It is now England's
busiest inland waterway, with
pleasure craft outnumbering
commercial barges. Fray's River,
a River Colne loop dug to power mills,
runs almost under Denham Deep
Lock which is, at 11 foot, the deepest
lock on the Grand Union.

Pass over the Denham Court driveway, guarded by kissing gates, into a meadow. On the far side, over to the left, there is the Denham Country Park Centre.

Continue to the end to find a kissing gate hidden in the hedge. Follow the wooden fence on the right and when this ends continue ahead with care over the golf course with the River Misbourne over to the left. On the far side, bear over to the fence on the left and reach a gate.

D The road is ahead and is reached by going right and left through another kissing gate. Turn right on Village Road, which runs into Denham passing Denham Church and the Swan and Green Man pubs.

Keep ahead at the green where the main street bears left. Ahead is Denham Place. At the end of the green, turn right into

Why are there ridges on the canal footbridge?

The Pyghtle. The wall of Denham Place is to the left and soon the golf course is to the right. On approaching the railway embankment, bear left with the main path for the tunnel where steps lead up to the platforms of Denham station.

A house in Denham

16 Marble Hill and Syon

START Twickenham
DISTANCE 4½ miles (km)
TIME 2½ hours
PARKING None
ROUTE FEATURES Towpath and stately home parkland

This Thames walk starts at Twickenham, where poet Alexander Pope is buried in the church. Tea merchant Thomas Twining lived next door, at Dial House. The riverside affords views of Richmond in its rural setting and two fine mansions. Each bank has cattle which vie for the claim to be the nearest herd to Trafalgar Square.

Go left out of Twickenham station to walk down London Road. At the junction, go ahead round Barclays Bank and past the end of Church Street to continue south down to the river.

Turn left, downstream, with the water on the right. Soon there is the Barmey Arms before the road curves to pass the church. Here, the road is separated from the river by part of York House garden. Pass Dial House and follow the walled road under a bridge. Just after passing under a second garden footbridge, go right to follow a path back to the river.

A After a playground, the path passes the ferry and the front of Marble Hill House. Soon there are views of Petersham Meadows and Richmond, as the river bends.

Marble Hill was completed in 1729 for George II's mistress, Lady Suffolk, and later it was briefly home to Mrs Fitzherbert, first wife of the Prince Regent. Its tiny interior has been compared to both Wilton House and Versailles. In one corner of the garden Hammerton's Ferry, started in 1909 by Walter Hammerton, links Marble Hill to 17th-century Ham House opposite. In the other, there is the country's largest black walnut tree.

PUBLIC TRANSPORT Rail to Twickenham and from Syon Lane
REFRESHMENTS Cafés at Marble Hill and Syon Park
PUBLIC TOILETS Marble Hill and Syon Park
ORDNANCE SURVEY MAPS Explorer (161 London South)

View of Richmond from Hammerton's Ferry

At Richmond Bridge follow the path up to the road just past the phone box. Cross over to walk down Willoughby Road, which leads to Ducks Walk. At the far end continue with the river under the railway and Twickenham Bridge to follow riverside Ranelagh Drive past the Richmond Lock.

B As the road bears inland, go ahead round the barrier on a to a

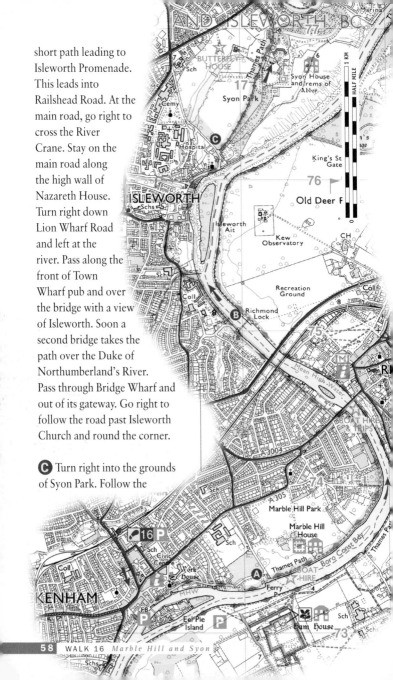

short path leading to Isleworth Promenade. This leads into Railshead Road. At the main road, go right to cross the River Crane. Stay on the main road along the high wall of Nazareth House. Turn right down Lion Wharf Road and left at the river. Pass along the front of Town Wharf pub and over the bridge with a view of Isleworth. Soon a second bridge takes the path over the Duke of Northumberland's River. Pass through Bridge Wharf and out of its gateway. Go right to follow the road past Isleworth Church and round the corner.

C Turn right into the grounds of Syon Park. Follow the

Twickenham riverside

? *What can you see behind the battlements on the roof of Syon House? You will need to stand back but be careful of the road.*

estate road ahead, passing the front of the house and then the shop and café. The road narrows to a passage used only by cyclists and walkers. At the main road, cross on the crossing and turn right. The road runs over the Grand Union Canal into Brentford.

Turn left up Market Place and go right and left round the White Horse pub. In the square, bear half right across the middle to go down the walled road opposite towards a house with a white front door. Turn right into Somerset Road. At the end, go left along a main road to see Brentford station ahead, by a crossing. For trains to central London continue on the road over the railway bridge and turn right down steps on the right by the King's Arms.

Syon House is home of the Duke of Northumberland. In 1553 Lady Jane Grey made her abortive bid to become queen from here and in 1616 Princess Pocahontas, who found London a dirty city compared to America, came to stay. Later, Charles I's children were brought here to escape a London plague. The Great Conservatory in the garden inspired Joseph Paxton to design the Crystal Palace.

17 *Epping Forest*

START Chingford station
DISTANCE 4 miles (6.4km)
TIME 3 hours
PARKING Bury Road car park next to golf course office
ROUTE FEATURES Firm woodland paths

Epping Forest is known as London's Back Garden, having been saved from development by the Corporation of London. When Queen Victoria arrived at Chingford station in 1882 she drove to High Beach and declared: 'It gives me the greatest satisfaction to dedicate this beautiful forest to the use of my people for all time.' Trees include England's largest forest of hornbeams.

Turn right out of the station forecourt and, when the buildings end, go left up Bury Road. Before the golf course café, go right by a gate onto a firm path. Where this turns left, keep forward with a ditch to the left.

åß On reaching a five-way path junction, turn left over the stream into a long straight path running through a wood. This is the Great Ride, open to horse riders.

? *What does the place name High Beach mean?*

High Beach Church

PUBLIC TRANSPORT Rail to Chingford
REFRESHMENTS Tea hut at High Beach and café next to Queen Elizabeth's Hunting Lodge
PUBLIC TOILETS None
ORDNANCE SURVEY MAPS Explorer 174 (Epping Forest & Lee Valley)

The first crossing is the wide Jubilee Ride. The way then rises and bends. Ignore a left turning but, at a fork, bear left and soon go over another cross ride at Almshouse Plain. The path now winds before climbing steadily, and steeply at one point, up through Hill Wood. Eventually, the way bends right to reach a gate by a road.

B This junction of forest roads is known as Cross Roads. *Only to visit High Beach Church, turn left along the road, forking left on the Lippitts Hill road.* The main walk continues to the right. After a short distance, turn right again to enter an unmarked side road known as Fairmead. There is a tea hut to the left (open Wednesdays to Sundays).

Follow the metalled road which has more horse than motor traffic.

The wooded lane runs downhill. Soon the trees to the left give way to Fairmead Bottom open ground and a view of Fairmead Pond.

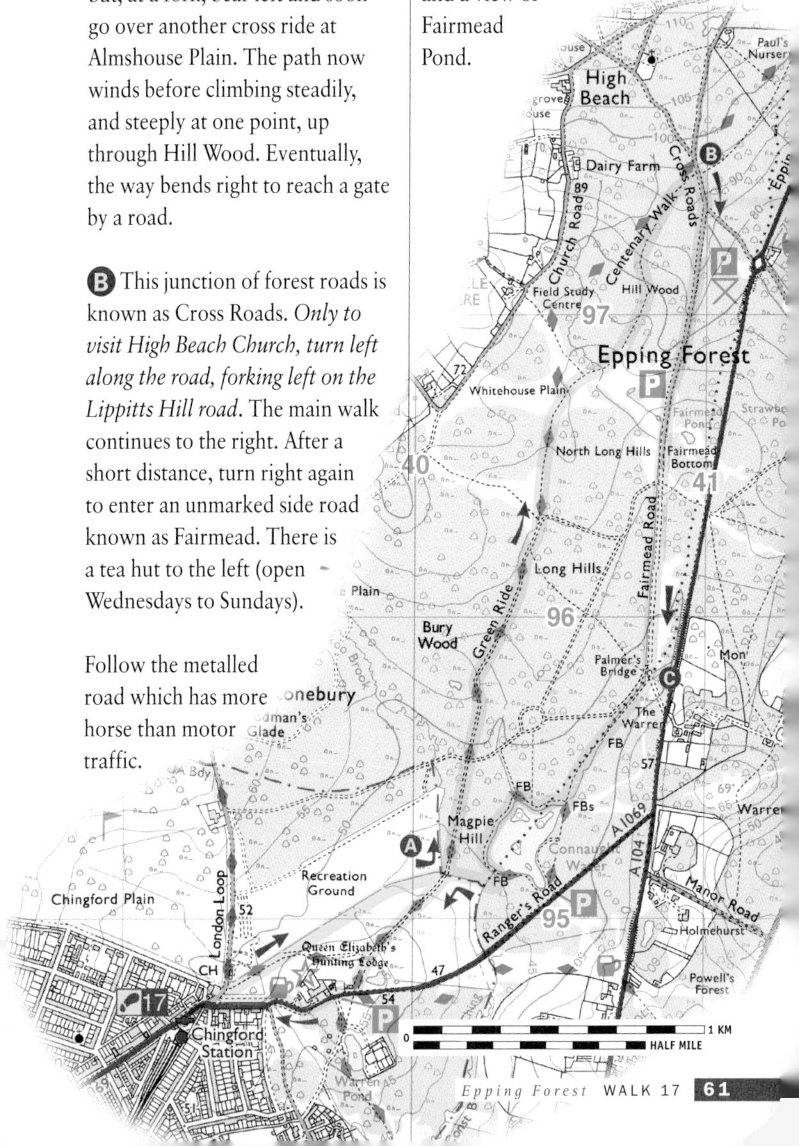

Map labels: Paul's Nursery, High Beach, Dairy Farm, Cross Roads, Church Road, Centenary Walk, Field Study Centre, Hill Wood, Epping Forest, Whitehouse Plain, Fairmead Pond, North Long Hills, Fairmead Bottom, Fairmead Road, Long Hills, Green Ride, Bury Wood, Palmer's Bridge, The Warren, Stonebury, Woodman's Glade, Plain, Magpie Hill, Recreation Ground, Connaught Water, Chingford Plain, London Loop, Ranger's Road, Queen Elizabeth's Hunting Lodge, Chingford Station, Warren Pond, Manor Road, Holmehurst, Powell's Forest, Strawberry, Mon, Warren

0 — 1 KM
HALF MILE

The hard surface changes to rough just before the easily missed Palmer's Bridge.

Queen Elizabeth's Hunting Lodge

C Cross the bridge over a stream and bear right on a woodland path which runs straight ahead. Later, Connaught Water can be seen to the right. Here, turn right to walk round the vast lake. The water is to the left. When on the third and south side, go right just before the outflow. Follow a short path, with water to the left, to a footbridge leading to open ground. At once, go right to find the five-way path junction crossed on the outward route **A**. This time, go half left on the green horse ride running uphill with a view of a building at the top of the hill.

The wide path gently climbs the hill to reach a viewpoint behind Butlers Retreat café. Go right along the road to pass Queen Elizabeth's Hunting Lodge and the Royal Forest Hotel. Follow the road downhill into Chingford. The station is on the left. ●

Connaught Water covers 8 acres and was created between 1883 and 1893 out of a small, swampy pool. The plan was to drain the Forest to encourage more pasture for cattle. It is named after the first Ranger of the Forest, the Duke of Connaught, who was Queen Victoria's son. Until recently, rowing was common in summer and skating on the frozen surface in winter. Now it is best known for its wildfowl and islands.

Queen Elizabeth's Hunting Lodge was built in 1543 for her father Henry VIII, who probably enclosed Chingford Plain for deer. The galleries would have been open to give a better view of the deer or even sometimes to allow for shooting from the high vantage point. But Elizabeth I is said to have come here to celebrate the defeat of the Spanish Armada by riding her horse up the stairs. The Royal Forest Hotel next door was built in imitation in 1880.

Brent River Park

18

START Hanwell station
DISTANCE 5½ miles (8.9km)
TIME 3 hours
PARKING Roadside parking outside the station
ROUTE FEATURES Riverside paths which can be muddy

Hanwell's church spire is seen by railway passengers on the Paddington line. It was a favourite view of Queen Victoria. Nearby, at Perivale, there is a much older but less known church nestling in riverside trees. The churches are linked by the Brent River Park where, on a quiet bank, herons can often be seen.

Go ahead from Hanwell station to follow the road round to the left. Turn left again at the end to approach the railway bridge. Bear right but keep to the left of the garden ahead to walk along the path below the railway embankment. Soon, the way is across the grass of Churchfields, with a view of the railway viaduct over to the left.

The path leads directly to Hanwell Church.

Ⓐ Turn left to the end of the road by the church and go right just before the lychgate entrance to

Hanwell's landmark church was built in 1841 on a site where there has been a church since the 12th century. Buried inside is umbrella inventor Joseph Hanway. Rectors have included Derwent Taylor Coleridge, son of the poet who lived in Highgate, and Harry Secombe's brother Fred.

Brent River Park. A path runs downhill to the River Brent. Cross the bridge and turn right. Keep ahead on this main path until the river swings back. At the next path divide, go right to keep near the water. The way is soon over grass. Cross the next bridge and turn right to keep as near to the water

PUBLIC TRANSPORT Train to Hanwell except Sundays
REFRESHMENTS Pub at Perivale
PUBLIC TOILETS Perivale Park
ORDNANCE SURVEY MAPS Explorer 173 (London North)

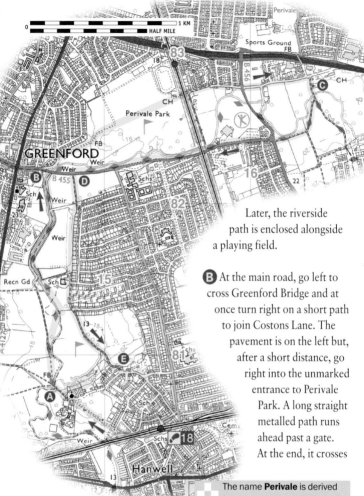

Later, the riverside path is enclosed alongside a playing field.

B At the main road, go left to cross Greenford Bridge and at once turn right on a short path to join Costons Lane. The pavement is on the left but, after a short distance, go right into the unmarked entrance to Perivale Park. A long straight metalled path runs ahead past a gate. At the end, it crosses

on the left as possible. Pass the next bridge to follow the grass waterside path. The way bends by an inlet. Here, there are steps leading to an alternative higher path which can be used when the river is in flood.

The name **Perivale** is derived from 'pear tree valley'. The church dates from 1135 and had a weatherboarded tower added in 1510. By 1900, the local population was still only 60. Tudor brasses commemorate the Mallet family whose name lives on with the Mallet Arms pub built on the site of Church Farm.

a stream and bears left with the water. At a sharp turn to the left, keep ahead over grass to pass trees to the right.

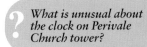
What is unusual about the clock on Perivale Church tower?

On the far side join a metalled path by a running track to pass under the railway. Follow the Stockdove Way road ahead and cross the main road to continue along Perivale Lane. The tall spire of St Peter's Ealing can be seen to the right.

At the Mylett Arms, go right at a lychgate to find Perivale Church down a narrow path.

C Continue along the path past the church and over a wooden bridge spanning the river. Go right on a fenced path through Ealing Golf Club and keep forward to eventually reach a main road. Go ahead, walking on the right hand side, along Ruislip Road East.

Beyond the sports centre, the river

reappears with a path running under the railway. After briefly returning to the road, the path resumes and slowly moves away from the road. Where the riverside grass is wide, and just after a short concrete stretch of river wall, bear

Perivale Church

The River Brent

over to a gate on the left to rejoin the road.

Cross the road on the nearby crossing to go down a fenced path opposite signed 'Hanwell'. At the end, go right through barriers to continue south on a gravel path. The way is through young trees with a brief view ahead of Hanwell Church spire. The path runs into High Lane which, beyond housing, continues as a rural road and, after passing a stables, runs uphill with a gravel surface.

E At the top, go past the gate and turn left along Church Road. The way bends by a small green at Cuckoo Lane to run gently downhill. At the bottom, go right into Campbell Road to reach Hanwell station and the starting point of the walk. ●

Mill Hill

19

START High Barnet
END Mill Hill East station
DISTANCE 5½ miles (8.9km)
TIME 3 hours
PARKING High Barnet Station or Stapylton Road car parks (pay and display)
ROUTE FEATURES Fields which can be wet and village street

Totteridge Fields and the surrounding area is old Hertfordshire countryside trapped between two Underground stations. Nearby Totteridge Church is still part of the Diocese of St Albans rather than London. This walk is across hay meadows with hawthorn and blackthorn hedges. There are beehives, blossom in spring and buttercups in summer before the hill top Mill Hill is reached.

At the top of the slope, leading up from High Barnet station, keep forward across the end of Meadway and up Barnet Hill. Bear left into Wood Street to pass between the church and Tudor Hall.

At the Register Office, go left into Old Court House Recreation Ground. Pass a pond and keep to the left of the bowling green ahead. Follow the long path behind running downhill to Mays Lane. Turn right and go left by the post box into Leeside.

A At the end of the road, follow a path to a junction before a bridge.

Elizabeth I, who often passed through Barnet on the way to Hatfield, founded the grammar school. General Monck put up at the Mitre on his way south from Scotland for Charles II's Restoration. Samuel Pepys dined at the Red Lion (now the Firkin), popular with Tories, while the Whigs gathered at the Green Man. The keyhole of St John's Church at the top of the hill is level with the cross on the dome of St Paul's Cathedral.

Turn right to walk on the grass between the houses and Dollis Brook. Keep forward through a gap and, at the end of the third field, go over a stile. Go right for a few yards and then left to enter another field.

PUBLIC TRANSPORT Underground to High Barnet
REFRESHMENTS Pubs in Mill Hill
PUBLIC TOILETS None
ORDNANCE SURVEY MAPS Explorer 173 (London North)

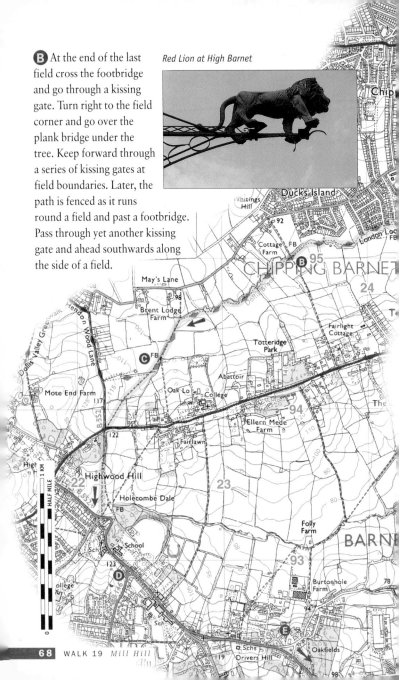

B At the end of the last field cross the footbridge and go through a kissing gate. Turn right to the field corner and go over the plank bridge under the tree. Keep forward through a series of kissing gates at field boundaries. Later, the path is fenced as it runs round a field and past a footbridge. Pass through yet another kissing gate and ahead southwards along the side of a field.

Red Lion at High Barnet

C At a junction in the corner, go through the kissing gate and bear half left across the corner of a playing field to a gap leading to Totteridge Fields nature reserve. Bear half right across the field. Cross a bridge and continue half right past a tree in the centre of the field. Go through a kissing gate to a road junction.

Cross over and go right for a few yards to find steps leading up to a kissing gate at a wood. A path runs ahead along the edge of the wood with a horse racing ground to the left. At the top, the path runs through another gate into a narrow strip which opens out into a sloping field. Keep forward, beyond the gate at the bottom, to a double kissing gate at a road.

Cross the road with care to pass between a green

Church Cottages at Mill Hill

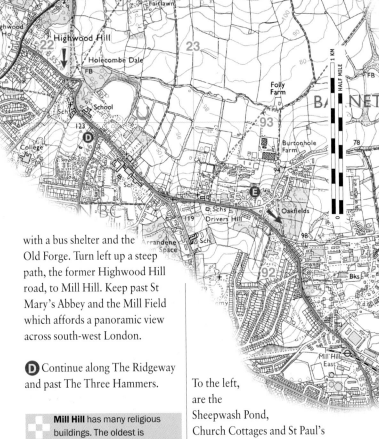

with a bus shelter and the Old Forge. Turn left up a steep path, the former Highwood Hill road, to Mill Hill. Keep past St Mary's Abbey and the Mill Field which affords a panoramic view across south-west London.

D Continue along The Ridgeway and past The Three Hammers.

> **Mill Hill** has many religious buildings. The oldest is Rosebank, a former Quaker meeting house; Mill Hill School was founded for Dissenters in 1807; Anglican St Paul's was built by reformer William Wilberforce in 1833 and the Roman Catholic institutions are in 18th-century houses such as Holcombe House which became St Joseph's College. The modern building is a Jehovah Witness centre. The almshouses by Angel Pond date from 1697. The landmark Institute of Medical Research was designed in the 1930s.

To the left, are the Sheepwash Pond, Church Cottages and St Paul's Church. There is a view of Angel Pond beyond the village sign.

E After the huge National Medical Research building, the road becomes Bittacy Hill running down to Mill Hill East station. ●

> **?** *What is the footpath at 3 Church Cottages in Mill Hill made from?*

Watford

20

START Watford
DISTANCE 5 miles (8km)
TIME 3 hours
PARKING Watford station
(pay and display)
ROUTE FEATURES Canal
towpath and woodland
paths

*Whippendale Wood once provided
firewood and game for a now demolished
mansion. A lime avenue was planted in at
least 1720 and predates the conifer and
broadleaf plantations to the north. 270 plant species have
been recorded, along with butterflies and woodpeckers. In
summer, the nature reserve near the canal and river are
bright with yellow and purple wild flowers.*

👣 Turn left out of Watford
Underground station to walk along
Cassiobury Park Avenue and bear
left into Swiss Avenue. At the
bottom, go left again into Gade
Avenue. On reaching the River
Gade, at the bend, leave the road
by going half right and across a
footbridge. The path runs between
the river and a lake before turning
left and meeting the end of
Rousebarn Lane.

Ⓐ On crossing the Grand Union
Canal, at once go right down onto
the towpath. Here, there are often
several houseboats moored. Follow
the canal, with the water to the

right, through the woodland. In
the trees on the far bank there are
watercress beds. After just over half
a mile there is a bridge at Watford
Lock.

Turn inland from the bridge and go
right on a wide path signposted
'Footpath 30' and running parallel
to the towpath. Stay on this main
path as it moves away from the
canal and then bends north-west
through the trees to become the

> **?** *What unusual road
> sign must drivers heed
> between Watford station
> and the River Gade?*

PUBLIC TRANSPORT Underground to Watford
REFRESHMENTS Cassiobury Park tea hut
PUBLIC TOILETS Cassiobury Park
ORDNANCE SURVEY MAPS OS Explorer 172 (Chiltern Hills East)

long lime avenue. Cross a metalled drive and look left for flying balls on passing over a golf course.

B At the end, where there is a junction, do not go ahead downhill but go right. This path is the boundary between Watford, to the right, and Hertfordshire's Three Rivers Council.

On reaching a car park, at once turn left. A woodland path runs gently downhill. At a divide, take the firmer way to the right to pass

Whippendale Wood

Houseboat at Watford

the pit. The path now falls and rises by a fence. There is a dip to pass Leeswood Cottages. Later, the path runs downhill with a view to the right of glasshouses and a treehouse. There is a modern cottage at the bottom of the hill.

C Before the gate go left, but not sharp left, and soon the way becomes stepped. Stay on this main path, ignoring all turnings. Eventually, there is a view to the right over a field as the path begins to run downhill alongside Rousebarn Lane. At the five-way junction at the bottom go ahead, to pass between the board with map and the gate, on a narrow path which bends through the woodland.

D At the T-junction, go left uphill on a footpath signposted 'Cassiobury Park'. At the golf course, first look right for balls and then, halfway across, left. The path continues ahead through woodland, over a drive and a second open space where flying golf balls come from the right. Keep downhill to reach Watford Lock.

Cross the canal bridge and the second bridge over the River Gade to enter Cassiobury Park.

Cassiobury Park is the 190 acre former grounds of the Earl of Essex's 17th-century mansion, which attracted landscape painter JMW Turner to produce several views. The castellated building was pulled down in 1927 and the grand staircase is now in New York's Metropolitan Museum. The park, which once included work by the famous English garden landscaper Humphrey Repton, has a narrow gauge railway.

Keep ahead on the main path which, after a bend near the golf and refreshments huts, runs through an avenue towards Watford's town centre.

E At the junction, go right on a path shared with a cycle lane. Take the next right, by tennis courts, to leave the park. The path becomes Shepherds Road. Turn right for Watford Underground station and the starting point of the walk. ●

Watford's parish church, dating from 1230, is one of Hertfordshire's largest churches. The town was once a stagecoach stop and nearby in the High Street is the 16th-century One Crown pub. The 18th-century house of brewer Joseph Benskin has become a museum. Expansion of the town came with the arrival of the canal and then the main line and Underground railways.

Further Information

Walking Safety

Although the countryside within the M25 and Greater London has few dangers care should still be taken. Some country paths, even in a London Borough, can be a distance from a road or house so Country Code rules should still be applied.

Paths can unexpectedly be wet and slippery and sensible shoes should always be worn. Comfortable shoes are just as important in the city where there are many more metalled paths. However, managed woodland and forest bridlepaths often have carefully laid surfaces which withstand both rain and horses' hooves.

Care should be taken when near rivers or streams. The Thames and River Lea can be dangerous if not treated with respect and walkers should always remain on the towpath or riverside path and not enter the water, however tempting on a hot day.

In warm weather, it is advisable to carry a drink and not rely on pubs always being open in the afternoon. Water is always best on a walk rather than a fizzy or orange drink. A plastic bottle almost filled with water and kept in the freezer overnight will melt slowly when carried in a rucksack on a hot day and provide a welcome cold drink before reaching a café or home.

Care is also needed when crossing the capital's very busy roads and in the city centre the visitor should be aware of possible traffic when stopping to look at a view or historic building. Where there is no pavement you should always walk on the right hand side of the road to face on-coming traffic.

Follow the Country Code

- Enjoy the countryside and respect its life and work
- Guard against all risk of fire
- Take your litter home
- Fasten all gates
- Help to keep all water clean
- Keep your dogs under control
- Protect wildlife, plants and trees
- Keep to public paths across farmland
- Take special care on country roads
- Leave livestock, crops and machinery alone
- Make no unnecessary noise

Hampton Court Palace

- Use gates and stiles to cross
  fences, hedges and walls
  (The Countryside Agency)

Useful Organisations
British Waterways
Willow Grange, Church Road,
Watford WD1 3QA.
Tel. 01923 226422
Fax 011923 201400
E-mail: enquiries.hq@

britishwaterways.co.uk
Web site:
www.britishwatewrways.co.uk

Countryside Agency
South East & London Region:
Dacre House,19 Dacre Street,
London SW1H 0DH.
Tel. 020 7340 2900
Fax 020 7340 2999
Web-site: www.countryside.gov.uk

English Heritage
23 Savile Row, London W1X 1AB.
Tel. 020 7973 3434
Fax 020 7973 3001
Web site: www.english-
heritage.org.uk

Epping Forest
Information Centre, High Beach,
Loughton, IG10 4AF.
Tel.020 8508 0028
Fax 020 8532 0188
Web-site:
www.cityoflondon.gov.uk

London Walking Forum
3rd Floor,
31–33 Bondway, London SW8 1SJ

Tel. 020 7582 4071
Fax. 020 7820 8208
E-mail: info@londonwalking.com
Web site:
www.londonwalking.com

Lee Valley Park
Lee Valley Park Information Centre
Abbey Gardens, Waltham Abbey,
Essex EN9 1XQ
Tel. 01999 2702200
Web site:
www.leevalleypark.org.uk

National Trust
Membership and general enquiries:
PO Box 39, Bromley,
Kent BR1 3XL

St John's Chapel at Hampstead

Tel. 0202 8315 1111
E-mail: enquiries@ntrust.org.uk

London Regional Office:
Hughenden Manor,
High Wycombe,
Buckinghamshire HP14 4LA
Tel. 01494 528051
Web site:
www.nationaltrust.org.uk

Ordnance Survey
Romsey Road, Maybush,
Southampton SO16 4GU.
Tel. 08456 05 05 05 (Lo-call)

Public transport
London Buses: 020 7222 1234
Railtrack: 08457 484950
Underground: 020 7222 1234

Ramblers' Assocation
2nd Floor, Camelford House,
87–90 Albert Embankment
London SE1 7TW.
Tel. 020 7339 8500
Fax 020 7339 8501
Web-site: www.ramblers.org.uk

London Tourist Board
Written enquiries only to
Glen House, Stag Place,
London SW1E 5LT
E-mail: enquiries@
londontouristboard.co.uk
Web site:
www.londontouristboard.co.uk

London Wildlife Trust
Harling House,
47-51 Great Suffolk Street,
London SE1 0BS.
Tel. 020 7261 0447
Fax 020 7261 0538
E-mail: londonwt@cix.co.uk
Web-site: www.wildlondon.org.uk

Local tourist information centres:
Camden: 020 7974 5974
City of London: 020 7332 1456
Harrow: 020 8424 1103
Hillingdon: 01895 250706
Hounslow: 020 8583 2929
Twickenham: 020 8891 7272

Youth Hostels Association
Trevelyan House
Dimple Road
Matlock
Derbyshire DE4 3YH
Tel. 01629 592600 (General
enquiries)
Web site: www.yha.org.uk

Public Transport
For all public transport enquiries:
Travel line: 0870 608 2608

*Ordnance Survey Maps of
North London*
Outdoor Leisure maps 160
(Windsor), 161 (London South),
162 (Greenwich), 172 (Chiltern
Hills East) and 173 (London
North).

Answers to Questions

Walk 1: Before Farringdon Street covered the River Fleet anyone walking down the lane had to turn again on reaching the water blocking the way.

Walk 2: It was the grand entrance to Euston Station demolished amid great controversy in 1963.

Walk 3: Dick Whittington's cat.

Walk 4: Since 1798, according to the blue plaque on the police station.

Walk 5: The Great Exhibition catalogue. The 1851 exhibition was held in Hyde Park.

Walk 6: The land was laid out as a park for the Prince Regent, the future George IV, acting as Regent for his father George III, who was believed to be mad.

Walk 7: Blue lamps usually found outside London police stations.

Walk 8: The first fatal road accident.

Walk 9: Horse riders.

Walk 10: The date on the side is 1887 which means that it was built in Queen Victoria's Golden Jubilee year.

Walk 11: It features the figure of Diana, the Roman goddess of hunting.

Walk 12: The Cow Byre. The original Victorian thatched building on the site was a cowshed. Byre means cow shed or hut.

Walk 13: Deer, according to the traffic signs.

Walk 14: A corner of land. This was a secluded spot on the marshy riverside.

Walk 15: To stop horses and bargees from slipping.

Walk 16: A lion which is the crest of the Duke of Northumberland.

Walk 17: Gravel bank. The area surface is made up of trees and grass.

Walk 18: It's a sun dial.

Walk 19: Upturned inkpots from Mill Hill School, which is why the cottage is called Inkwell.

Walk 20: Beware of frogs.